America's GREAT CATS

America's GREAT CATS

Text by Gary Turbak
Photographs by Alan Carey

NORTHLAND PUBLISHING

To Joey and Liza, the littlest cougars.

First Edition 1986

SECOND PRINTING 1991

ISBN 0-87358-409-0 softcover

Library of Congress Catalog Card Number 86-60513

Composed in the United States of America

Printed in Hong Kong by Lammar Offset Printing Ltd.

Library of Congress Cataloging-in-Publication Data

Turbak, Gary.
America's great cats.

1. Cougars. 2. Bobcat. 3. Lynx. 4. Felidae.
5. Mammals—North America. I. Carey, Alan. II. Title.
QL737.C23T79 1986 599.74'428 86-60513
ISBN 0-87358-409-0

3-91/5M/0326

CONTENTS

INTRODUCTION

THE WORLD IS MADE UP OF TWO KINDS OF PEOPLE—those who are cat people and those who are not. If you're a cat person, you know it. And so does the feline with whom you share life. If you're not a cat person, perhaps this book will help you to become one.

This book is about North America's big cats—cougar, bobcat, and lynx. If you've ever laid eyes on one of these animals, the day was probably quiet, the glimpse fleeting, and the moment special. America's great cats are like that: mysterious, ethereal, ghostly, quick, and oh so special.

It's more likely, however, that you've never seen a cougar, lynx, or bobcat outside of a zoo. Don't feel bad. Thousands of loggers, ranchers,

"Raw power,
perfectly controlled."
Adult lynx

biologists, and other frequenters of wild land spend their entire lives in the woods without ever coming face to face with one of these cats. I have never seen a wild bobcat or lynx, and the only cougars I've met were sent my way by a pack of hounds. But it doesn't really matter that we rarely get to see the great cats. The important thing is that we know they're there.

From a window in the office in my home, I can look west toward an unimpressive lump of earth called Blue Mountain. Pines and spruces cover the slope, and here and there are the bald spots where the trees have not yet caught hold. The only thing special about this mountain is that it's visible over the top of my computer screen—that and the cats that must surely live there. It seems impossible that there, almost within shouting distance of a busy city, live the cats. Not lynx, perhaps, for they're not common in Montana, but certainly bobcats and cougars.

I've never seen one of the big cats on Blue Mountain. I probably never will. It's sufficient just to know that sometimes, in the shadows of dusk, felines on huge paws still creep across the land. To know that these great hunters have adapted well enough to my presence—and to yours—to linger close. To know that despite the havoc we humans have wreaked upon the Earth, the great cats still find it a good place to live.

Like barometers that show us what the weather fronts are doing, the cats tell us that the woods are still, in some sense, wild. They tell us that we are not in complete control—that part of the world, especially at night, belongs to them.

How Shall We Know Them

Scientists call the cat family *Felidae,* from which we get the common term feline. Long ago, cathood diverged into two groups, one that cast its lot with mankind and one that chose to dwell in woodland secrecy. But the eons have scarcely touched the bonds between the two. The cats of this book are but big versions of the diminutive creature that lies curled at your feet. The character core is the same. Poodles and dachshunds bear little resemblance to the wolves from which they sprang, but the cat stalking a mouse in the field across the street is a nearly perfect reduction of the cougar hunting deer on that distant hillside. They are forever kin.

But what makes a cat a cat? From the neck backward, a cat's skeleton is much like that of a dog, and most people would be hard pressed to tell one from the other. The big difference lies in the skull—short and round in the cat and elongated with a well-developed snout in the dog. It's this short snout that gives the jaws of a wild feline the tremendous crushing power needed to snap the neck of an animal many times its own size.

" . . .the apex of predatory evolution."
Bobcat

A cat has thirty teeth, including four of the most highly developed canines in the carnivore world. Though a cat can hold its victim in a viselike grip, it lacks effective grinding and chewing teeth and a jaw that can move sideways. Consequently, cats gulp their food whole, depending upon a strong digestive system to process the largely unchewed fare.

Because its rear legs are so highly developed, a cat has fantastic leaping ability. Based on your height and the cat's, the casual leap your tabby makes to the bookshelf might be equivalent to you springing from the ground to the top of a three-story house.

Other features are peculiar to cathood. Facial whiskers help locate obstructions in its path. Claws can be retracted for silent stalking. The rough tongue has evolved to scrape all the meat off bones. A cat, which hunts by sight and hearing, has large eyes and ear folds that gather sound. Binocular vision (present in most predators) permits precise focusing.

Cats also are the only animals that purr, and only recently have scientists learned how it's done. When a cat wishes to utter its normal vocalizations, it does as we all do—forces air past tense vocal cords that vibrate to create the sound. When it purrs, however, the vocal cords (really thin folds of tissue) open and close several times a second, not unlike rapidly operating elevator doors. When they are closed, air beats against them to create a purr. All cats purr, and no one is certain why, although the sound seems to be a friendly signal.

But a cat is certainly more than the sum of its parts. Nature has breathed into felines a spark of magic that has propelled them to the apex of predatory evolution. If you have a cat as a roommate, you're acquainted with feline strength, agility, and intensity. You know that cats are at once silly and wise. Cautious yet fiercely brave. One minute that fluffy ball of fur lies asleep in its favorite chair. . . and the next moment some inner sentinel has sounded the alarm, putting every muscle on instant full alert.

You know, too, that a cat is its own being, really more a partner than a pet. Cats are loners, associating with people or other cats just enough to get what they need—and always on their own terms. They are independent and aloof, in charge of their own lives. So, too, are the wild cats. "Raw power perfectly controlled," is how one biologist described them to me. They are, quite simply, the world's supreme hunters.

I write this book because I am a cat person. I know at least a little of the beauty, strength, and mystery that is feline. And I write with the hope that there will always be Blue Mountains, always be a place for the great cats. Perhaps a little of what I say will stick, and maybe somewhere down the road it will make a difference.

COUGAR

COUGAR
Lithe and Splendid Beasthood

Felis concolor, the only wide-ranging, long-tailed cat of North America.

IF YOU'VE SEEN ENOUGH GRADE B MOVIES, YOU MAY think you know the cougar:

The moon shimmers forth, flooding the rimrocks with light and shadows. At first nothing stirs, but then one of the shadows appears to move. With perfect fluidity, a cougar issues forth from the rock itself and melts into the night.

On silent feet the cat travels. Its ears lie back, and its green eyes reflect the moonlight. Stealth is in the cat's every movement. For perhaps half a mile the cougar walks, making no sound.

In an open spot on a ridge, the cat pauses. It tilts its head back slightly and twists its neck to one side. The cat's lips part, and its white fangs glow. Then it screams. A terrifying, elongated, piercing scream. For three or four seconds, the sound of that terrible voice echoes across the valley. Then silence.

In the pasture below, the cattle instinctively close ranks. The heads of the deer in the meadow jerk upright, eyes wide with fear. A small boy cries softly inside the farmer's cabin, and his mother double-bars the door. The farmer eyes the rifle resting on the rack above the fireplace. No living thing is safe. The cougar is about.

That has long been the cougar's image. It is part fact, part fancy, part fear, part myth. It has dogged the cougar for centuries and has grudgingly given ground only in the last couple decades.

Today's cougar is the descendant of a Pleistocene predator that specialized in small prey and left the horselike herbivores to the much larger saber-toothed tiger. Over the millennia, the huge hooved animals became smaller or vanished, and the saber-toothed tiger passed from the scene. But the smaller cat, the cat without stripes or spots, prospered.

Thus began the reign of one of the most adaptable mammals on earth. Ranging from northern Canada to Patagonia and from the Atlantic to the Pacific, the cougar became the most widely distributed mammal (other than man) in the western hemisphere. The same species that prowled the South American tropics eked out a living for itself in the Yukon woods. From the red-rocked deserts of Utah to the alpine meadows of British Columbia to the forests of New England, the cougar thrived.

Because of its wide distribution, the great cat acquired many names. Settlers east of the Mississippi called it panther, painter, or catamount (short for cat of the mountains). In Florida, the animal is still known as the panther. Latin Americans call it *el leon.* In most of the United States where the cat still lives, it goes by puma, mountain lion, or cougar. Cougar, which is a French corruption of a Tupi Indian word, seems to be the most widely accepted and will be used exclusively throughout this book. To scientists, the big cat is known as *Felis concolor,* cat all of one color. The important thing to remember is that, regardless of the many names, there is only one wide-ranging long-tailed cat of North America.

Today, the cougar's range and numbers in North America have been greatly diminished. Pushed before the European tide that swept across the continent, the cat retreated to the wilderness. When that wilderness disappeared, the cat moved on again. In North America, the cougar now lives in the eleven western states, Texas, British Columbia, and Alberta. A remnant population holds out in the swamps of Florida, and small breeding populations may exist in Minnesota, Michigan, Wisconsin, and Manitoba. Occasional sightings are made in other states and Canadian provinces. Few, if any, exist in Alaska.

Independent, shy, and secretive, the big cats are impossible to count. Each adult stakes out a home range that may, in the summer, cover hundreds of square miles. At prominent locations along the edge of this range, the cat scrapes together small piles of leaves, pine needles, and twigs. When soaked with urine, these seemingly insignificant "scrapes" act as boundary markers. Transient cougars typically change course and leave the area when they encounter another cat's scrape. Within its home range, a cougar is almost constantly on the prowl, sometimes traveling as much as thirty miles in twenty four hours. Only females with young set up housekeeping in a den.

Occasionally, territories may need to be defended, but usually the signposts are sufficient to keep itinerants on the move. Each cat respects the other's territorial rights. This technique, called mutual avoidance, probably evolved along with the cougar's solitary life style. Because it hunts alone and cannot depend on a pack for sustenance, the cougar can ill afford an injury sustained in defending its territory. It is to every cougar's advantage to allow each cougar its private domain.

When two cougars do come together, it usually is for mating, which for the female happens every two years; breeding may take place during any season. For about two weeks, the male and female travel together, copulating several times. Then they part company. The male plays no part

"Independent, shy, and secretive. . ."

" . . . spotted kittens are born in a cave, rock crevice, or beneath an uprooted tree." *Left:* Mother and three-week-old kittens; *right:* Five weeks later, a cub bounds across the snow.

in rearing the young that are to come.

Three months later, from one to six (usually two or three) spotted kittens are born in a cave, rock crevice, or beneath an uprooted tree. At birth, the kittens are blind, weigh a pound or less, and are a foot long. In two weeks, their eyes open. In two months, they leave the den. In six months, their spots disappear, and they become *Felis concolor*—cats all of one color.

Abandoning the den, the female resumes travel within her home range, teaching the kittens the hunting skills they'll need to survive. Though the young may come to outweigh their mother, they remain with her until they are about eighteen months old. At that time, the female drives them off to establish territories of their own. A young cougar may need to travel a considerable distance before it finds suitable range not already occupied

Cubs at eight weeks.

Mother and cubs at the water.

by one of its kind. In a year or two, the youngsters will themselves breed. Cougars live about ten to twelve years in the wild.

An adult male cougar weighs about one hundred sixty pounds, and the female about twenty-five pounds less. The largest cougar on record, a male shot in Arizona, tipped the scales at two hundred seventy-six pounds. The only larger feline in the Americas is the jaguar. From nose to tail tip, the cougar can measure eight feet.

The big cat's normally tawny coat ranges from reddish to chocolate brown, depending upon where it lives. Parts of the muzzle; the backs of the short, round ears; and the tip of the tail are black. Its whiskered face is like that of the housecat, only proportionately larger. And it purrs. The huge tail—as big around as a man's forearm—is used for balance. With rear legs longer than forelegs,

Powerful legs drive a slender, supple body.

the cougar walks with hindquarters slightly elevated. Vertical leaps of eighteen feet and horizontal ones of forty-five feet have been reported. The cat also is a good and agile climber.

With powerful hind legs driving a slender, supple body, the cougar is the epitome of successful carnivore evolution. Retractable, needlelike claws stud its padded feet; canine teeth are long and sharp; powerful jaws can snap a deer's neck. The cougar is the unquestioned lord of its environment and every inch the picture of "lithe and splendid beasthood" that naturalist Ernest Thomas Seton called it decades ago.

The big cat has few natural enemies. While many predators can and will attack unprotected kittens, adult cougars fear no four-legged animal. The only larger carnivore in North America is the bear. In areas where the continent's three largest predators—wolves, bears, and cougars—coexist, each is probably quite happy to avoid the others. Only man poses any significant threat to cougars.

And if it were not for one behavior quirk, the cougar might be completely invincible. That quirk is the cat's innate, overriding fear of a barking dog. One or two dogs, even large ones, would stand little chance against a cougar if the cat were to stand and fight. But it does not. Instead, the cougar runs, and—ridiculous as it may seem—a vociferous ten-pound poodle can send a one hundred sixty-pound cougar scrambling for the trees. Woe to the dog, though, that confronts a cougar and forgets to bark.

Why the cougar runs from a barking dog remains something of an evolutionary mystery. Somewhere deep in the feline's past, an animal that barked probably preyed upon cougars. Wolves perhaps, or another form of canine that evolution left behind. At any rate, today's cougar retains a fear of barking dogs.

This fear helped America's settlers extirpate the cougar from the land they wanted for their crops and herds. Because they feared and misunderstood the cougar, the Europeans who peopled the United States and Canada sought to destroy it. Indiscriminate killing and habitat destruction caused the cougar population to plummet as the human horde moved west across North America. By 1900, the big cats had virtually disappeared from the eastern half of the continent. Only in the vast expanse of the West did the cougar find refuge, but even there its days appeared to be numbered. And no one mourned the demise of the "big horse-killing cat, destroyer of the deer and lord of stealthy murder with a heart craven and cruel," as Theodore Roosevelt once referred to the cougar.

But that was yesterday. The cougar of today has shucked its old image as neatly as an elk drops its antlers. The modern cougar is protected and cherished, not persecuted. Frequenters of wild places now thrill, not cringe, at the sight of a cougar. The big cat has truly pulled off a major wildlife surprise—and victory.

Making A Living

Few people have been privileged to witness a cougar killing its prey, but anyone who sees the rhythmic, flowing movement of an adult cougar on the run knows intuitively that the cat is a predator to the core of its being. It has been called the quintessential hunter, the walking epitome of successful carnivore evolution.

Deer and elk make up most of the cougar's diet, although it will eat mice, squirrels, hares, and other rodents—including porcupines, which it flips over and kills by attacking the quill-less belly. Raccoon, coyote, and even grasshopper may also be on the menu. The cougar rarely touches carrion, preferring instead to eat only the prey it catches itself. Infrequently, cougars will kill livestock. For some unknown reason, most livestock predation occurs in the southwestern United States. In most other parts of cougar territory, such attacks are extremely rare.

Like all cats, whose sense of smell is less developed than that of canines, cougars hunt primarily by sight and hearing. The big cat can prowl at any time, although most kills probably take place at night, because that's when most prey animals are active. Contrary to popular misinformation, cougars do not lurk in the treetops waiting to ambush passers-by. The cougar stalks its prey on the ground, moving slowly through its territory until the flick of an ear, the twitch of a tail, or the sound of breathing tells it that game is nearby.

Then the approach becomes intense. On silent feet the cat moves forward, sometimes putting its hind paws in the marks made by the front ones to lessen the chance of a twig snapping or leaf rustling. If the cat has more than one deer or elk from which to choose, it selects a specific individual to attack—perhaps the closest one, one off by itself, or one that exhibits the abnormal behavior of a sick or injured animal.

When the cat has crept close to the unsuspecting prey, it attacks in a few lightning-quick bounds. Leaping onto the back of the deer or elk, it may attempt to puncture the prey's neck vertebrae with its huge canine teeth, or perhaps pull the animal's head upward until the neck snaps. It may also use its claws to rip open the ungulate's throat. Usually, death is mercifully swift: the prey may die with a few strands of browse still between its teeth. Occasionally, a cougar's stalk is so successful that it kills a deer right in its bed.

Though a cougar can hit forty miles per hour in short spurts, it has a relatively small lung capacity and little endurance. If it does not capture the prey in a few seconds, the cat gives up and looks elsewhere for a meal.

Up close, it's easy to see why the cougar is such an efficient predator. Its one and one-half inch-long canine teeth and powerful jaw muscles

Death is mercifully swift for this mule deer.

can instantly snap a bull elk's neck. The thick, inch-long retractile claws on its front feet can shred the thickest hide and rip the windpipe from a deer's throat in seconds. "The cougar is an extremely efficient killing machine," says one cat researcher. "Even when it's relaxed, the cat's entire body feels like one huge, tensed, steely muscle."

But finding a meal is not always an easy chore for the cougar. It's likely that every successful stalk is preceded by two or three failures. And getting its paws on the prey is just the beginning. Biologists have come across cougar-prey battlegrounds where four-inch pines have been snapped off like matchsticks. Cougar researcher Wilbur Wiles learned firsthand that the big cats don't always come out on top when they go hunting:

Deep in the winter wilds of Idaho, Wiles followed the tracks of a female cougar that he had captured and marked with an eartag just two days earlier. Soon, he came upon a wildlife drama written in the snow. The cougar had stalked to within a few yards of a small herd of grazing elk. Selecting a young bull as her victim, the cat rushed the elk and leaped onto its back. Together, the two animals slid down a steep slope and smashed into a tree. The elk escaped.

A short time later, Wiles' dogs treed the cougar, but because the researcher had just examined it two days earlier, he did not drug the cat for study. Three weeks later, however, he came across the same animal again and decided to have a closer look. As soon as he had tranquilized the cougar with a drugged dart and lowered her to the ground, he could see that something was terribly wrong. The cat's jaw was broken, and two of her canine teeth had been ripped from her mouth. Puncture wounds from the elk's antlers dotted her shoulders and hips. Reluctantly deciding that the cougar could not survive, Wiles shot the sleeping animal. The elk had won.

One of the most detailed descriptions of a cougar kill was recorded several years ago by officials in Canada's Banff National Park. Though no one witnessed the attack, the story in the snow was clear: On a slight slope, the cougar approached three or four elk. The elk bolted, and the cougar followed, leaping on a bull and causing it to stumble to its knees. For one hundred fifty yards, the elk thrashed and bucked down the hill with the cougar clinging to its back. Then, losing its grip, the cougar found itself being dragged through brush and over logs, holding on only by its front claws. Somehow, the cat regained its position atop the bull and continued the ride, probably biting and clawing at the elk's neck. About two hundred fifty yards from the initial point of attack, the elk went down, its neck finally broken.

Even seasoned wildlife experts are greatly impressed with the cougar's strength. "I've worked with elk," says one, "and there's no way three or even four men could control a healthy adult elk. Yet, a single cougar—which weighs no more than an average man—can attack and kill a bull elk. The cats simply are amazing."

The cougar may well be the most efficient and effective hunter in the animal world. African lions rarely prey on animals more than three times their own size; the jaguar (which is larger than the cougar) seldom kills anything bigger than a deer; and the great tiger of India usually outweighs its prey.

The cougar, however, will attack virtually any prey. Settlers called the cat a "horse-killer," probably with some justification. Before the bison disappeared from the plains, some of them became cougar prey. And researchers recently have discovered that in some areas moose make up much of the cat's diet.

The cougar's documented hunting ability is unparalleled. In Canada, a hundred pound female cougar killed a five hundred pound moose. In Idaho, a female cat weighing ninety-eight pounds stalked and killed two six-point bull elk that probably weighed six or seven times as much as she did. Once the prey is dead, the feats of strength may continue. Cougars frequently move their kill, and it's not unheard of for a cat to drag a five hundred pound elk several yards across level ground.

As soon as it has made a kill, the cougar eats and wanders off to nap in a secluded spot. Before it leaves, however, the cat may cover the prey with sticks, grass, and other forest debris to hide it from scavengers. If the kill is left undisturbed, the cat may continue to feed on the carcass until almost nothing is left.

A common misconception is that cougars wreak havoc on elk and deer herds. It's true that these ungulates do provide most of a cougar's sustenance, especially in winter when other prey may be scarce. Although a cougar may kill a deer every two weeks or so, it does not necessarily follow that the deer population suffers from having cougars around.

Cougar experts say that predation by the big cat won't have much of an effect on deer and elk populations if the herds are generally healthy. Typically, the cat will kill an animal that is very young, very old, lame, diseased, or otherwise less fit. These, simply, are the easiest prey for a cougar to catch. So, in a sense, the cougar doesn't select its own prey. Nature does it for him.

Wildlife managers now know that cougars (and other predators) are good for deer, elk, and other prey species. Besides removing the weak and diseased from the herd, cougars keep the ungulates somewhat scattered, which helps prevent overgrazing and overbrowsing. And by holding the prey species in check, cougars help prevent overpopulation and the resulting massive die-offs from widespread starvation.

Getting Along With Man

If humans had not happened upon the scene, the cougar's reign might have been almost without boundary. For eons, the big cat freely roamed the continent, paying only occasional heed to fellow hunters, the grizzly and wolf. The strong, swift, adaptable cougar seemed virtually invincible. But there came that dark day in cougar history when the long, narrow tracks of man first appeared in the streamside mud of North America. The life of the cougar has not been the same since.

Aboriginal people developed an ambivalent relationship with the big cat. While they feared the cougar's ability to attack and kill even the strongest among them, they admired its hunting skill. The animal's silence and stealth lent an aura of mystery to the uneasy early relationship between men and the beast, and the warrior who killed a cougar received much acclaim.

Sometimes, the cougar became part of the culture. Aztecs and other Indians attempted to heal their sick with cougar bones, paws, and gall. In New Mexico, two immortal stone cougars still stand as testimony to the esteem in which the cat was once held by the Cochite Indians. In a Cheyenne tale, a mythical cougar comes to the Indians as a kitten suckling at the breast of a woman; later, the grown cat provides meat for the band. Various tribes held the cougar's hunting ability in awe while fearing the cat's lethal claws and teeth.

But the restless truce between cougar and mankind came to a sudden end when Europeans set foot on American shores. With the possible exceptions of the serpent and the wolf, no creature in history has been so maligned and misunderstood as was the big cat in the days of American exploration and settlement. Each human generation handed down to the next a hatred of the cunning, bloodthirsty, unpredictable killer cougar.

True, the cat killed the deer that settlers wanted for food. And it sometimes slew their livestock. And a few settlers probably died at the jaws of a cougar. But hatred of the cougar went far beyond economics and personal safety. It was the cat's personality the settlers despised. The cougar was secretive and mysterious, and the people feared what they could not see. Men who had never laid eyes on a cougar knew in their hearts that if they ever saw one they would kill it. To them, the cat had no redeeming value.

As myths grew up around the cougar's strength and stealth, the cat was blamed for countless crimes it did not commit and credited with feats it could never have accomplished. Otherwise reasonable settlers believed the cougar could kill a horse with one blow. Many people said they knew someone who supposedly had seen a cougar leap a fence with a colt in its mouth. Around the campfire, cougar tales grew until the cats were making lat-

Newspapers proclaimed the presence of killer cougars. Schools closed. Bands of armed men scoured the woods. Lumberjacks strapped on pistols, and armed guards stood watch over forest crews. Businesses offered rewards for cougar skins. No one seemed to care that the guilty cougar was already dead or that no sailor had been reported missing.

Then one day, a man in sailor garb came to the police and identified the cloth scraps and buttons. His jacket had become soaked with whale oil, he said, and he had tossed it in the garbage. The "man-eating" cougar had been guilty of nothing more than plundering a garbage can. Fortunately, only three cougars were slain in the purge that followed the jacket's demise.

Only in the West, with its mountains and inaccessible terrain, did the cougar survive, but here, too, its eradication seemed imminent. In the 1950s, cougar slayers were still front page news. Returning hunters, proudly displaying dead cats across their automobile hoods, were given a hero's welcome. As recently as the early 1960s, some states dispensed a fifty-dollar bill to the killer of each cougar.

But the scent of change was in the air. The environmental movement of the 1960s emphasized the primacy of natural systems. People who had never thought about such things before realized that virtually everything in nature had a place, a purpose. The age-old idea that wild creatures were either good or bad (depending upon how they affected humans) fell into disrepute. People began to accept the notion that wild species had a value in and of themselves, that animals like the cougar had a right to exist. Thoughtful people began to see predators as important components of a new concept called an "ecosystem."

Also, the science of wildlife management was maturing about this time. Improvements in radio telemetry and tranquilizing drugs now allowed biologists to gather huge amounts of information on virtually any species. Scientists scrutinized predator-prey relationships as never before, and they came away with a new understanding of the predator's role. They learned that predators frequently do not kill as much game as local folks believe and that the animals they do kill often are those less capable of perpetuating the herd. In the 1920s, wildlife biologists thought that the elimination of all predators from the Kaibab Plateau in Arizona would be good for the deer population. With the cougars, wolves, and coyotes gone, the mule deer increased from three thousand to thirty thousand animals, destroyed the range, and brought on mass starvation. By the 1960s, the biologists knew better.

All this augured well for the cougar. First British Columbia, then Florida, then a rush of provinces and states scrambled to remove the big cat from their varmint lists and eliminate bounties. In 1965, Colorado became the first state with a significant number of cougars to eliminate bounties. States now spend money to study and protect cougars, not reward people for killing them.

Most western states reclassified the cougar as a game animal, which meant hunting could be closely controlled. California even went so far as to impose a complete (but temporary) moratorium on all cougar hunting. Cougars today can be hunted in eleven western states. Typically, a hunter may kill one cougar per year, although several states allow sportsmen with dogs to pursue and tree additional cougars as long as these cats are shot only with a camera. Only Texas does not protect its cougars with a regulated hunting season.

Just as predation can be good for an elk herd, controlled hunting is good for the cougar. In addition to making the cougar wary and fearful of humans, hunting keeps the cougar in the public eye. It allows wildlife managers to control the population, and it generates income for managing the cats.

Cougars are hunted in the winter with dogs, which chase the cat up a tree and keep it there until the hunter arrives. Because shooting a cougar out of a leafless tree is not a challenge, many sportsmen are turning to catch-and-release hunting, in which the only trigger that gets pulled is the shutter on a camera. Men and dogs walk away, and the cougar is free to go—to be hunted again another day.

The elimination of bounties and uncontrolled hunting have sharply reduced the number of cougars killed each year. Professional cougar hunters, who once shot thirty or forty cats per annum, are no longer devastating the cat population. Consequently, cougar numbers are climbing. California claims twenty-four hundred cougars; New Mexico and Arizona, twenty-five hundred each; Washington, two thousand; and Alberta, one thousand. Some states and provinces do not make official estimates, so there is no consensus figure for all of North America, although one guess is that there are twenty thousand cougars north of Mexico. There is no question, however, that cougar populations in the western part of the continent—and the cougar's image almost everywhere—are quite healthy.

Few conflicts remain between people and cougars. In the southwestern United States, the cats prey on livestock (primarily sheep) often enough to raise the ire of ranchers. However, in other livestock-producing areas, such as Idaho, the cats and ranchers live largely in harmony. Studies currently underway in the Southwest may eventually help eliminate the livestock predation.

About the only other black mark on the cougar's record is the rare attack on a human. Though the paranoia of a century ago has all but disappeared, some people still harbor a fear of cougars. Although documented attacks are few, and human deaths at the jaws of a cougar extremely rare, press coverage of these incidents often helps distort public perception of any real problem.

Records are sketchy, but it is likely that since 1900, cougars have killed no more than about a dozen people in Canada and the United States. Most of these have been children, which the cat probably perceived as some type of prey. A few other people have been mauled by cougars, but the cat repeatedly has shown that it prefers to flee from human encounters. In fact, most people living in cougar country pass their entire lives without ever laying eyes on a cat. Statistically, anyone venturing into cougar territory has much more to fear from insects, falling trees, and lightning than from cougars. You are much more likely to be attacked by a dog while jogging on a city street than by a cougar in the woods. Attacking humans simply is contrary to the cougar's nature.

Still, it does happen. While snowshoeing alone just before dusk near Banff National Park in Alberta, Scott Udall, a young Banff resident, turned and saw a cougar crouched seventy five feet away. Instantly, the cat bounded to within five feet of him but stopped when Udall screamed at the animal. A life-and-death game of cat and mouse followed.

Udall fell on his back in the snow, raising his snowshoes in defense. As the cat circled, he pivoted to keep the shoes between himself and the cougar. Knowing that the cat might soon challenge this weak defense, Udall removed the snowshoes and began using them as sword and shield as he edged his way toward some trees.

The cat laid its ears back, bared its fangs, and pawed menacingly at Udall, but the snowshoes kept the animal at bay. Once, when Udall struck the cougar smartly in the face, the cat lashed out with lightning speed, but it still did not rush in for the kill. Eventually, the young man scaled a thickly branched pine that proved too difficult for the cat to climb. The cougar then wandered off into the woods, and Udall walked nervously back to town in the growing darkness.

But incidents like this are rare aberrations in the cougar's otherwise secretive lifestyle. Most people now know that they have nothing to fear from the great cat. In the twenty-five years since the cougar began wearing its new cloak of respectability, it has made the almost miraculous transition from vermin to valued species. People whose grandfathers would have shot a cougar on sight now thrill at the glimpse of one. Of course, it is the people, not the cougars, who have changed.

The Cougar Chasers

The sound of baying hounds echoes through the forest southwest of Calgary, Alberta. Ahead of the dogs runs a cougar. Following behind, through the knee-deep snow, trudge three biologists.

The sun is but a pink glow in the west when the cat is finally treed twenty-five feet up a slender spruce. Group leader Orval Pall quickly loads the capture gun with a drugged dart and fires, but it is too dark to see if the animal is hit.

Now things happen fast. In five or six minutes, the 175-pound male cougar should be out cold. Pall must climb the tree and attach a rope to one of the cougar's hind feet so it can be lowered to the ground for study. If he gets to the animal before the drug takes effect—or if the dart missed—he could face an angry cat with razorlike claws. If he arrives too late, the drugged animal could fall and be injured.

Pall dons climbing spurs, flips on his headlamp, and quickly ascends to a point just below the cougar, which by now is but a silhouette against a darkening sky. He still cannot tell what effect the drug has had.

The cougar's long tail hangs within reach, and Pall decides to use it to test the animal's status. He tugs the tail with the gentleness of a surgeon, but it is too much, and the cougar tumbles from its perch. Instinctively, Pall cradles the cat in his arms and pins it against the tree with his body. Their heads are four inches apart. The cat's jaws are open. Its huge teeth shine like sabers in the dim glow of the headlamp. In a great, brief moment of uncertainty, Pall's gut tightens and adrenaline floods through his body. Then he notices the telltale glaze in the cougar's eyes. "Please, please be out," begs the biologist.

And the cougar accommodates him. Like a very large infant, it dozes on in his arms. Pall attaches the rope, and the cat heads down.

Pall, a young researcher with the Alberta Fish and Wildlife Division, is one of several dedicated scientists who have helped unlock the secrets of the cougar's life. Without the information they gather, the North American public might still perceive the cougar as a "big horse-killing cat . . . with a heart craven and cruel." Though much has been learned about the cougar, biologists throughout the West continue to probe into every corner of the cat's life so that the animal's future might be secure and that conflicts with humans might be reduced.

Cougar study is a curious mixture of ancient techniques and modern technology. The traditional method of hunting with dogs is still the best way of locating cats; were it not for the cat's innate fear of barking dogs, cougar study would be next to impossible. Typically, a researcher looks for a cougar track in snow, then releases hounds to pur-

As recently as the 1960s, some states dispensed a $50 bill to the killer of each cougar.

sue and tree the animal. If the cougar does not give the dogs the slip, it eventually will seek refuge in a tree.

Eons of evolution apparently have taught cougars that an arboreal sanctuary is totally safe. A treed cougar, looking as out of place as a crow in a birdbath, often settles down to wait calmly for the barking intruders to leave. The treed cougar that hisses, paws, and spits is largely a figment of the moviemakers' imagination. The big cats have even been known to fall asleep in a tree while men and dogs milled around down below.

The eons, however, have not taught the cougar about guns, and it is a relatively easy mark for the scientist shooting a drugged dart (or the hunter firing a lethal bullet). On impact, the dart injects a tranquilizing drug into the animal's bloodstream, and in a few minutes, the cat is out cold. Before it can fall and be injured, a rope is attached to one leg, and it is lowered to the ground.

The cat will be out for ninety minutes, and there is much to do in that time. First, the biologist pulls each of the animal's lower eyelids away from the eye and squeezes an antiseptic salve from a tube onto the inside of the lid. By gently closing the cat's eye, he spreads the salve over the entire eyeball. This will keep the eyes from drying during the time that the cat will be unconscious and unable to blink.

With a tape, the researchers (usually two or

three work together) measure the cat's length and girth. They roll back the cat's lips to expose its teeth, which they measure with calipers. The amount of yellow staining on the white enamel and the degree of gum recession provide a general indication of the cougar's age, but there is no way to determine it exactly.

Heart rate, respiration, temperature, and the size of paws, claws, and skull are all recorded. A blood sample is drawn, and the cat is checked for parasites and injuries. The biologist then turns his attention to the dart that still hangs from the animal's rump. He tugs on the dart to determine the location of the barbed tip beneath the skin, then makes a tiny incision with a sterile knife to free the dart. An antiseptic is put on the wound.

Next, the biologist attaches a radio collar to the cat's neck—loose enough so that it will not interfere with the animal's eating or breathing, yet tight enough so that the cougar cannot pull it off. Attached to the collar is a small transmitter that will emit a radio signal for up to three years. In the future, biologists will be able to locate this cat by pinpointing the origin of the signal coming from the collar. By keeping track of the cat, they can plot the animal's territory, monitor its hunting success, find its den, and reexamine it at nearly any time.

Radio telemetry has come a long way since its inception a couple of decades ago. A radio collar can tell researchers whether a cougar is moving or at rest and what its heart rate is. An unmanned monitor can plot a cat's periods of activity and rest over twenty-four hours. The collar can be rigged to inject another tranquilizing drug dose at a preset time or via a radio signal from a researcher. If the biologist is collaring a young cougar whose neck might grow and cause the collar to become too tight, a portion of the collar can be set to rot through and fall off after a few months.

When the work has been done and the data recorded, a rope is attached to all four of the cougar's feet, and the cat is lifted off the ground to be weighed. Then the cougar is left comfortably resting, and the researchers retreat about twenty-five yards to await its recovery. As the cat comes out of its stupor, huge tears roll from its eyes, an involuntary reaction to minor irritation. It also may vomit in reaction to the drug. Moments later, the cat wobbles to its feet and walks unsteadily off into the woods.

When conditions permit, tracking cougars from the air is the most efficient way of monitoring radio-collared cats. Once every week or so, a cougar researcher may spend several hours in the passenger seat of a single engine plane bobbing in the updrafts over his study area. Beside him lie topographic maps, and on his head are earphones that pick up the signal emitted by a cougar's collar. Because each cat broadcasts on a different frequency, individual animals are easily identified. Each wingtip carries a radio receiver antenna, and by switching from one to the other, the biologist can chart a direct course toward any cougar he may have collared.

When a cat's position is located as closely as possible from two thousand feet above the wooded ground, the pilot drops to two hundred feet and puts the plane into a steeply banked circle. By gauging the intensity of the radio signal coming from earthward-pointed wing, the researcher can pinpoint the cat's location to within a couple hundred yards. As soon as one location is marked on the map, the pilot climbs, the radio frequency is changed, and they're off for the next cat. The cougars, which like to spend their days resting beneath low-hanging spruce boughs, are rarely seen. Later, the researcher will plot the day's locations alongside previous ones to determine a home range for each cougar.

That's how cougars are studied today. In the 1960s, when the first in-depth cougar research began, things were different. Radio telemetry was an emerging science, and there was virtually no previous data on cougars to provide a research base.

In 1963, Maurice Hornocker was a young biologist just out of graduate school at the University of Montana. Before heading off into the wilds of Idaho to study cougars, he sought to perfect capturing and drugging techniques. To do so, he paid Montana houndsmen fifty dollars to call him when they had a cougar treed.

One winter day the call came in, and Hornocker headed for the woods. It was dark by the time he got there, so the men, dogs, and cat settled in for the night.

At dawn, Hornocker fired a drugged dart into the cat's hip, sending the animal scrambling for the top of the towering pine. Immediately, Hornocker strapped on climbing spurs and started up. The drug was supposed to tranquilize, but not knock out, the animal, and if all went as planned, the cat would not resist as Hornocker slipped a rope around its foot and lowered it to the ground. When he was about fifty feet off the ground, Hornocker looked above him to the cat perched ten feet away. The cougar snarled, and Hornocker realized that the drug dose had been inadequate.

Afraid that the partially drugged cougar might jump or fall on him, Hornocker decided he may be safer above the cat than below it. He climbed rapidly, keeping the tree trunk between himself and the cougar. As he drew even with the animal, the cat reached out with a front paw and took a half-hearted swipe at him around the trunk.

As it did, its tail flopped around the other side of the tree. Instinctively, Hornocker grabbed it. With the cat's own movement adding leverage, Hornocker swung the cougar by the tail out into the air. Like a giant flying squirrel, the cat glided unhurt into the soft snow below. High in the tree, Hornocker shook with fright. He had just launched a cougar. . . and a career.

Though he had no way of knowing it as he clung high in that pine, Maurice Hornocker was to become a world-renowned wildlife researcher and the premier authority on cougars. The information he has gathered about the big cats has helped remove the cloak of mystery and suspicion from the public's perception of the animal. Through his speeches, articles, and films, he has helped convince the public that the cougar should be treasured, not despised.

Hornocker chose to do his cougar study in some of the wildest terrain in the lower forty-eight states, the Idaho Primitive Area (now the River of No Return Wilderness). To assist him, he hired veteran woodsman Wilbur Wiles. The purpose of Hornocker's work was to shed some light on the reclusive cat by studying births, deaths, territoriality, mating, effect on game species, and a host of other aspects of cougar life.

Hornocker and Wiles set out to do nothing less than capture all the cougars in two hundred square miles of rugged wilderness—capture them not once but many times. Because radio collars had not yet been perfected for use in such a wilderness setting, they could not track a cat's movements from a convenient ridgetop or airplane. They could determine a cat's home range only by capturing the animal again and again. Experts told them it was impossible.

In 1964, little was known about the cougar. Many people still believed the cat to be a wanton killer of deer and elk, and many states still paid a bounty to hunters who killed them. Myths abounded. "I heard stories about cougars carrying yearling colts in their mouths while they leaped over ten-foot fences," recalls Hornocker. "Of course, that's impossible, but because there was no one to refute such tall tales, cougar myths prospered."

In the fall of 1964, Hornocker and Wiles established several camps five to nine miles apart in the roadless study area, equipping each with sleeping bags, firewood, food, tent, and other necessities. As soon as tracking snow covered the ground, they set out with their hounds to tree and capture cats. Day after day, the two researchers climbed steep wilderness mountains, often through several feet of snow. Frequently, each night was spent at a different camp, depending upon where the day's tracking had led them.

Extreme cold and deep snow made life difficult in the Idaho wilderness. One night, with the temperature about 35° below zero, Hornocker and Wiles shivered with cold inside their sleeping bags. In desperation, they broke open hay bales an outfitter had left at their camp and called the dogs. Men and hounds made it through the night by snuggling together under a blanket of hay.

Beginning at two months of age, cougar cubs leave the den to explore their surroundings.

Sometimes three weeks would pass between visits to their base—a wilderness ranch on the edge of the study area—where they treated themselves to a bath, bed, and precious evening spent listening to the radio. Only once every month or so did Hornocker return to civilization to spend a couple days with his family.

Each time the two men captured a cougar, they measured and examined the animal, recording as much information about the cat as possible. Then they marked it for future identification with tattoos, tags, collars, or streamers, and let it go. The markers did not interfere with the cat's hunting, and many cougars were caught repeatedly over the course of the study.

For five consecutive winters, the pair lived in the Idaho backcountry. Wiles and graduate students spent five more years there, with Hornocker joining them part of the time. They walked thousands of miles and captured sixty-four different cougars more than three hundred times. Three cats that had been present at the beginning of the study were still there at the end.

As the data rolled in, Hornocker began putting together the pieces of the cougar puzzle. He learned that the cats are highly territorial creatures, with each cat staking out for itself a defined home range that is almost always avoided by other cougars. Young cougars typically migrate out of their mother's territory to find a home of their own.

He also learned that cougars pose no threat to healthy deer and elk populations. "The idea that cougars are wholesale killers of big game animals is a myth," he says. "With proper management, we can have thriving populations of deer, elk, and cougars." Time has proved Hornocker correct. Today, elk populations are increasing throughout much of the West, and deer numbers recently have been at record highs. There also are more cougars.

Now in his mid-fifties, Hornocker remains the dean of cougar researchers. He also has studied bobcats, lynx, and is currently involved with a cougar project in the Southwest.

The Search In The East

As forests fell before the axe, humans moved into almost every valley, and deer populations dropped, the cougar quietly disappeared from the eastern United States. The last cougar bounty in the East was collected by a New York hunter in 1890. Early in this century the consensus was clear: the cougar had vanished from the East. Or had it?

As the decades of this century ticked by, infrequent cougar reports kept alive a glimmer of hope that the cat may yet prowl the eastern woods. Now and then—in North Carolina, Alabama, Pennsylvania, Tennessee, and other states—someone would drive into this town or that with a dead cougar laid across the hood of his car. But were these animals part of a breeding population, escapees from a roadside menagerie, or refugees from Florida (where a small population of the cats survived)? No one could be certain.

In the mid-1970s, after the eastern cougar had been classified as an endangered species, the search for an answer speeded up. Dedicated researchers took to the backroads to find irrefutable proof that the big cat had never left the East. Wanted posters went up in hundreds of truck stops and country stores asking people to report every sighting of a panther (which is what the cats are called in much of the East). Researchers set out bait stations, carefully surrounding the bait with a moat of sand to record the cougar's track. At strategic spots along forest trails, self-tripping cameras waited to take a cougar's picture. Dedicated volunteers scooped promising looking scats into plastic bags and shipped them off for analysis.

But the search proved to be like chasing a ghost. Plenty of people called to report a sighting, but invariably their cougar turned out to be a bobcat, dog, or even a housecat. The hidden cameras took lots of pictures of bears and deer, but no cougars. The best that scientists could do with scats was to say that some samples *might* have come from a cougar. In one infamous incident, plaster casts were made of cougar tracks and a researcher was photographed holding the casts. When the photo appeared in *Smithsonian* magazine, it didn't take long for someone to notice that the paw prints were those of a dog, not a cougar.

For some inexplicable reason, many of the reported sightings were of *black* cougars, which have never been known to exist. The researchers can only guess that people had seen too many old movies with black panthers. And pranksters occasionally confused matters, sometimes by making perfect tracks with a dismembered cougar, and once by planting in a likely location the remains of a cougar that had died in captivity.

Sometimes, though, evidence for the presence of cougars appeared overwhelming. On one occasion, cougar searcher Bob Downing was called in

Mountain lion cub peeking out from between mother's legs.

to investigate a deer kill in North Carolina that had been made by some large animal. The one hundred pound carcass had been dragged more than one hundred yards and buried with forest debris as cougars are wont to do. At one place on the trail, it appeared that the predator had picked the deer up and carried it in its mouth, a feat no bobcat could perform. Still, no indentifiable tracks or scats were found, and the incident had to be filed with the many others that have question marks behind them.

The most encouraging reports come from Great Smoky Mountains National Park on the Tennessee–North Carolina border. There, maintenance workers saw a cougar chasing deer, picnickers watched a female and two kittens cross the road, and a retired animal trainer followed a cougar family and provided a detailed and accurate description. But there has been no photograph, no dead cat, no irrefutable evidence.

So, the quest goes on, conducted mostly by volunteers and die-hard cougar searchers. Much of the steam has gone out of the search, however. Although he still investigates promising leads, researcher Downing has retired from his position as chief cougar-seeker. Once optimistic that a breeding population existed in the East, Downing is reluctantly ready to admit that cougars there may be only transients.

Still, conditions are right for a cougar presence. Forests logged a century ago once again cover much of the East, and deer populations have increased. And what if Bob Downing or some other searcher discovers a breeding population? Will making the cat front-page news kill it with attention? Or should the secret be kept while the cougar inches its way back from near-extinction in the East?

In Florida, the picture is somewhat brighter. Biologists have long known that the panther never completely gave up life in the watery wilds of south Florida. Some estimates go as high as one hundred animals, but the people fighting desperately to save the great cat say there probably are between thirty and fifty panthers in the state. The cats dwell primarily in the sub-tropical habitat along the edge of the 570,000-acre big Cypress National Preserve and in Everglades National Park.

Panther hunting has been forbidden in Florida since 1958, but as people and their machines enter what once was wild land, pressure mounts on the cats. New subdivisions and roads chew up habitat, modern recreational vehicles penetrate even the most forbidding swamp, and agriculture and oil exploration eat up more panther territory. Some cats are shot illegally, and accidental road kills are a big problem. In one eighteen-month period, three panthers were killed along desolate Route 29 on the west edge of Big Cypress National Preserve. And it now appears that genetic inbreeding has given some male panthers a low sperm count and reduced chance of producing offspring.

Despite all this, researchers are cautiously optimistic about the cat's future in Florida. Since 1976, scientists have been trying to learn as much as possible about the cat's needs and numbers. Twelve panthers have been radio collared, and several agencies are cooperating well with the study. Additional habitat has been protected, and the highway that once killed many panthers is now equipped with passages that allow the cats to cross unseen beneath the road. It will be a long time before anyone knows for sure, but it appears that the Florida panther may have been saved from extinction.

LYNX & BOBCAT

LYNX & BOBCAT

Twin Phantoms

A lynx stands silhouetted in the early morning mist on Flathead River, Montana.

THE OTHER TWO LARGE NORTH AMERICAN CATS, THE lynx and bobcat, seem at first glance to be virtually identical. . . spitting images of each other . . . kitten cousins. But now and then, the mirror image they seem to reflect waivers out of synchrony, and we see two distinctly different creatures. Running through their personalities and lifestyles are wide chasms that make them as different from each other as dawn is from dusk. At crucial points in their ecology, the look-alikes take different paths through the woods, and that has made all the difference.

Let's begin with the physical. Like the cougar, the lynx and bobcat make themselves known to man in fleeting glimpses. A blur there in the trees.

A head bobbing through the brush. Now and then, a stationary figure poised in the shadows, then gone. A feline phantom.

Given only momentary, infrequent sightings and the fact that the two species are virtually never found together, it is difficult even for experts to say whether the cat they've just seen is a lynx or a bobcat. Both animals have long legs, short bodies, a stubby tail, a ruff of hair surrounding the face, and thick fur in mottled hues of grey, brown, buff, and black. Pointed tufts rise from the tips of their ears. An adult male lynx weighs about twenty-three pounds and the female four or five pounds less. In each case, a typical bobcat may be a few pounds lighter, but there are areas where bobcats are bigger than lynx. And to say that the lynx usually is larger, has longer legs, a shorter tail, or more pointed ear tufts (all of which are true) is not of much help when trying to identify a single animal.

Even the names are confusing. Scientifically, the lynx is called *Lynx canadensis,* indicating that it lives primarily in Canada. "Lynx" is a combination of a couple of Greek words that mean "lamp" and "to see" (possibly chosen because of the light reflective qualities of many cats' eyes). But the bobcat is *Lynx rufus,* rufus referring to the animal's sometimes reddish-brown color. In various places, however, the bobcat is known as the bay-lynx, and lynx-cat. The common name "bobcat" prob-

Lynx canadensis (lynx)

Lynx rufus (bobcat)

ably refers to that animal's short tail, although the bobbing motion it makes on the run may have had something to do with the nickname. The lynx also is called *loup-cervier,* and the name "wildcat" can refer to either one, although it's more commonly applied to the bobcat. Confusing, yes?

There are, however, identifiable physical differences, subtle though they may be. Look first at the feet. If they appear normal—like those of a housecat, only proportionately larger—the creature is probably a bobcat. If the feet appear disproportionately large, like those that might belong to a cartoon cat, you're probably looking at a lynx. Next, study the tail. On a lynx, the entire tip is black, while the bobcat's appendage is black on top and white underneath.

However, the most foolproof way to tell the difference between a lynx and a bobcat in the field is to look not at the animal but at a map. With few exceptions, the ranges of the two animals do not overlap. The lynx is largely a creature of the mature boreal forests of Canada and some of the northern woods of the United States. The bobcat prefers the more moderate climate of the United States and generally exists in Canada only in the southern extremities of the provinces. It is as if the two creatures took a map of North America, drew a line from coast to coast through southern Canada, and divided the continent between them: bobcats to the south, lynx to the north. There is, of course, a band along this line that may be home to either (and sometimes both) of the cats, but a large, short-tailed cat in Missouri will be a bobcat; in the Yukon, it's a lynx.

The bobcat got here first. Native only to North America, the bobcat was probably already well established when the lynx, a European, strolled across the Bering land bridge during the Pleistocene six hundred thousand years ago. Close relatives of the lynx remain in Spain, Sweden, Poland, Greece, Russia, and a few other places in the old world. Lynx and bobcats do not interbreed.

Both cats are skilled predators, feeding primarily on rodents, birds, and occasionally on larger prey such as deer. Both depend upon their keen sight and hearing; their sense of smell is secondary. They may, like the cougar, culminate a stalk with a short, furious rush. Or, they may lie in ambush along a rabbit trail waiting to capture a meal in a single pounce. Like other cats, both have razorsharp, retractile claws. Both utter the usual array of cat sounds at a volume proportional to their size. Although extremely shy, both species are rather curious, and curiosity can indeed kill the cat. Anything from brightly colored ribbons to after-shave lotion can lure them into traps.

As you might guess, breeding and reproduction are quite similar between the two species. Both produce only one litter per year, usually consisting of two to four kittens. The young, which are born with soft fur, weigh less than a pound, and their eyes don't open until they are several days old. Most litters are born in late winter or early summer (after a gestation of about nine weeks), although bobcats have been known to breed at almost any time of the year. In both species, the job of raising the young is left almost exclusively to the mother.

Much has been made of the personality difference between the two species. By reputation, the lynx is a shy, retiring, almost wistful creature that shuns humans at all costs. The bobcat, however, is perceived as a fierce fighter, a rowdy, an aggressor. Trappers say a bobcat in a trap will lunge and hiss at its captor, and if it were suddenly to come free would probably attack with hell's fury. A trapped lynx, on the other hand, strains quietly to get away from the approaching human. Researchers report that a lynx in a trap sometimes can be pinned to the ground with only gloved hands and given a tranquilizer with a hand-held syringe. A bobcat must be drugged from a distance.

No one is certain, of course, why such similar creatures have demeanors so different, but there is one theory. The lynx evolved in the frigid north where it was probably the only large predator capable of getting around in deep snow. It had virtually no natural enemies and almost no competition for prey. It had no need of an aggressive

Top: Bobcat kittens at nine weeks, near Glacier National Park; *bottom:* Lynx kittens

personality. The bobcat of the more temperate climate, however, evolved among wolves, coyotes, and bears. Without a stormy disposition, it might not have survived.

As we will see later, these personality differences—along with one seemingly unimportant biological difference—play a huge role in the separate ranges the two cats have staked out for themselves. For now, though, let's consider them individually.

The Bobcat

On the soft forest duff, feet make no sound. Here and there, the woods open onto mountain meadows, then quickly close again in thick brush. The day is hot, the trailside creek inviting, and you kneel to drink from the stream. As you lower yourself to the water, something forty feet away across the creek catches your eye. A form in the jumble of undergrowth. A splotch of color that doesn't quite fit.

As your gaze sharpens, you suddenly make out the pointed ears and unblinking eyes of a bobcat. For a few seconds, you ponder one another. Then, literally as you blink, the cat is gone. There has been no sound. The tangle of downfall looks right again. The colors blend. And you wonder if the cat was really ever there at all. But yes, you know it was. And that brief, ephemeral communion is about as close as you can ever hope to come to a bobcat.

Consider yourself lucky. Though the cat often lives and hunts in close proximity to humans, few people ever get a glimpse of it. But anyone who spends much time away from cities and towns probably has been close to the cat without knowing it. According to one unverified report, a young man in the West once posed his girlfriend beneath a tree in bobcat country, then backed off and shot a picture. They thought nothing more about it until the pictures were developed and included a bobcat nestled in the branches above the lady's head.

A bit of mystery has always surrounded the bobcat. Some North American natives and European immigrants believed that eating bobcat tenderloin could cure headaches. They put its fur on open cuts and its dung on skin eruptions. Held against the abdomen, its paws supposedly cured cramps, and its testes guaranteed a pregnant woman a healthy baby. Some people even believed that bobcat urine turned to precious stones. That's why the cat was always so meticulous about burying it, it was theorized.

Historically, the bobcat has ranged from the Yucatan to southern Canada and from the Atlantic to the Pacific. Human settlement of the continent has not been particularly hard on the bobcat, and it still occupies most of its original range. All of

Opposite: "Bobcats are the most numerous, most successful large cat in the Americas."

Dens under fallen trees
are common for bobcats.

the contiguous states except Indiana and Ohio have bobcats. It is not plentiful in the Northeast and Midwest, but it probably never was. Experts guess that there are between 700,000 and 1.5 million breeding adult bobcats in the United States, with a few thousand more in Canada.

It is the bobcat's adaptability that has made it the most numerous, most successful large cat in the Americas. In many places, the cat remains the largest predator, hanging on where the grizzly, wolf, and even the cougar were long ago eliminated.

It is at home in all types of terrain: the swamps of Florida, the deserts of Utah, the mountains of Washington. Where the best sanctuary available is a rocky crevice high on a steep slope, there the bobcat dens. But it might also seek refuge in a depression at the base of a stump, under a pile of human-cut brush, or in the appropriated meadow den of a woodchuck. When hares abound, the bobcat hunts hares. When that becomes difficult, it adaptably switches to mice, squirrels, gophers, an occasional porcupine, and a rare lamb or chicken.

Or wild birds. In the predawn gray of a Montana morning, grouse researcher Jonathan Hartzler nestled into his blind at the hilltop dancing grounds of the male sage grouse. Each May, for untold generations, the colorful birds had been coming to the same spot to perform their ritual mating dance. But grouse and scientists were not the only ones who knew about the place. At the first hint of

Hares are a favorite food.

light, birds began arriving, and Hartzler strained to see them just a few yards away. Suddenly, he heard a thump, sounds of flushing grouse, then silence. Through binoculars, he could see, twenty yards away, a bobcat walking off with a grouse in its mouth.

Bobcats also have been known to kill deer, but usually only when easier prey is not available or when the deer is crippled or otherwise easily dispatched. Attacking and killing a healthy adult deer that can weigh more than one hundred fifty pounds is a rather ambitious undertaking for a bobcat that usually will not hit twenty-five pounds wringing wet.

It does happen, however. One evening in Yosemite National Park, a ranger looked up from his work in the saddle room to see a four-point buck racing down the road past the government barns. Atop the deer perched a bobcat, teeth sunk into the buck's neck and claws anchored in its flesh. As the ranger watched with jaw agape, the duo disappeared from sight, and the outcome of the battle was never determined.

Because predation on deer and livestock is relatively infrequent and attacks on humans virtually unheard of, the bobcat's public relations battle has not been as difficult as that of the cougar. Even in the days when all predators were in disrepute, the bobcat did not inspire fear and loathing in the hearts of men. Though disliked and in many places bountied, the bobcat escaped the purge that forced the cougar to retreat into the inaccessible West. The bobcat today has a bounty on its head only in a few Texas townships.

Depending upon the vagaries of the fur market, the bobcat's reputation alternated between that of a pest and a valuable furbearer. Today, eleven states protect the bobcat, but hunting and trapping are allowed in the thirty seven others where the cat exists. (Alaska and Hawaii have never had bobcats.) About ninety thousand bobcats are harvested every year, but this regulated kill appears to be having no harmful effect on the overall population. In some places where they are heavily trapped, adjacent wilderness areas seem to supply cats that migrate into the trapped area to replace those that are killed. In California, for example, trappers have for years been taking about one hundred bobcats out of a single canyon each year. The value of a bobcat pelt today ranges from fifteen dollars to three hundred dollars, with the average price falling nearer the lower figure.

The bobcat has acquired a solid reputation as a cantankerous brawler. Like virtually all cats, it heads for the nearest tree when pursued by dogs. But few dogs, even though they may be two or three times the bobcat's weight, are a match for the feisty cat. In a one-on-one battle, the bobcat invariably emerges the victor. Likewise, the frontiersman who boasted that he "could lick his weight

Bobcat kittens.

Above: Whether on the ground or *(opposite)* in a tree, bobcats move with grace.

in wildcats," certainly would have had an unpleasant surprise if he ever tried.

In the wild world, bobcats have few enemies. Cougars probably kill a few, as do wolves and coyotes, although a tree provides an easy escape from the canines. Sometimes, though, danger comes from an unexpected source. In West Virginia early in this century, a fisherman happened upon a female bobcat with two small kittens. About the time he sat down to watch them, the cat came on the alert, grabbed one of her young loosely in her jaws and sprang into a chestnut tree. Depositing her baby there, she leaped to the ground and rescued the other kitten just as a wild razorback boar charged the tree, followed by a sow and litter of piglets.

With her young safely off the ground, the bobcat descended to a low branch just out of the reach of the raging boar, which likely could have killed the feline in short order. But the cat had no intention of tackling the razorback. Instead, she waited until one of the rabbit-sized piglets, which were calmly feeding on chestnuts, passed almost beneath her. Before the snorting boar could react, the cat hit the ground, grabbed the piglet, and streaked off into the brush. The razorback followed in hot pursuit. Over the rocks and logs they flew, the cat always just in front of the hog. A couple hundred yards away, the bobcat dropped the dead piglet and leaped to a ledge, leaving the boar foaming

and fulminating over its dead offspring.

Meanwhile, the sow and her young—perhaps feeling vulnerable without the boar present—wandered off into the brush. A moment later, the bobcat reappeared, took her young from the tree, and disappeared quietly into the forest.

Like the cougar, each bobcat establishes a home range that largely defines the cat's travels during its twelve-year lifetime. Typical bobcat habitat includes plenty of cover (woods, canebrakes, brush), travel routes (ravines, creek bottoms, ridges, old roads), open areas (clearcuts, meadows, bare slopes), and prey. Frequently, farms and livestock also fall within the cat's home range, but unless it attacks sheep or poultry, humans may not even be aware of its presence.

Though home ranges sometimes overlap, they usually are exclusive property. And a few "No Trespassing" signs, in the form of scent markings, feces, and urine-soaked scrapes, are all that are needed to keep neighbors and transients away. Bobcats rarely fight to defend their territory. The size of a bobcat's home range can vary from one to sixty-five square miles, depending upon the availability of prey. Youngsters driven out of their mother's territory have been known to travel one hundred miles in search of a home of their own.

During hard times, however, the cats may compromise, as researcher Ted Bailey discovered. A general decline in rabbit populations followed by a month of wind, snow, and subzero temperatures created a crisis for one group of Idaho bobcats. With most places of refuge covered with snow, four adult cats (two males and two females) abandoned their hermitlike lifestyle and "agreed" to share the same rockpile den. Each animal claimed a particular section of the rocks and had nothing whatsoever to do with its neighbors just a few feet away. Each hunted on its own, preying on a local concentration of jackrabbits and traveling no farther than about half a mile from the den. The uneasy truce held for two weeks, then the weather improved and each of the reluctant roommates went its own way.

Opposite: A bobcat fixes his intent gaze on a shadow across the snow-covered clearing.

The Lynx

In winter, dark comes early in the north country. The uneasy sleep of a wary predator ends, and the lynx moves from its bed of snow. Heat from the cat's body has melted the snow, and soon a shallow icy bowl will remain to prove that a lynx slept here.

In the twilight, the lynx walks silently across the deep and endless cover of snow, its large feet acting like snowshoes to keep it from sinking. Soon it comes to a trail through the woods, a trail used by snowshoe hares, the food that the hungry lynx now seeks. But lately, hares have been increasingly difficult to find, making life tough for a predator that does not easily switch to other prey.

Now and then, the lynx stops momentarily, sits on its haunches, looks and listens. Its sense of smell is not particularly keen, but a hare's slightest sound or movement will bring the cat to full hunting alert. Another half-mile passes, then the lynx stops cold in its tracks. In the oppressive stillness of the silent forest, the cat has heard a sound. Perhaps the gnawing of rodent teeth on bark. Perhaps the slightest crunch of snow under foot. The lynx peers intently into the brush as though it could see through solid wood. For several minutes, not a muscle moves in its taut body. Finally, the cat's sharp eyes spot the telltale twitch of a hare's ear fifty feet away.

In classic feline fashion, the lynx begins its fluid approach. Minutes more tick by as the cat cuts the distance in half. Suddenly, the hare senses danger, its eyes flare wide with fright, and it lurches to full speed in a single stride. But the lynx is moving, too. For twenty yards, the hare eludes its pursuer with sharp turns and spurts of speed, but they are not enough. A huge, clawed paw reaches out and pins the hare to the snow. An instant later, the cat's powerful jaws clamp onto the hare's neck, and the episode is ended.

First, the lynx opens the hare's chest cavity and eats the lungs, heart, and other organs. Over the next several hours, the cat strips the carcass of virtually all meat, leaving only the feet, jaw, and intestines untouched. As dawn starts to brighten the sky, the lynx strolls off a few yards to make a bed in the snow. For the cat, it has been a good night.

Like most predators, the lynx has known hard times. The cat once occupied much of the forest land in Canada and Alaska, parts of most northern states, and the Rocky Mountains as far south as Colorado. During the first half of this century, however, overtrapping eliminated the cat from much of its U. S. range and large sections of southern Canada. But during the 1950s and 1960s—due in part to better management and low fur

Opposite: " . . .the lynx walks silently across the deep and endless cover of snow. . ."

The eternal partnership:
lynx and snowshoe hare.

prices—the lynx reclaimed much of its original territory. Today, the cat lives in every Canadian province and territory except Prince Edward Island. Many of the northern tier of states have lynx, but the populations are small.

The lynx continues to play an important economic role as a furbearer. It is heavily trapped in Canada and Alaska, and four other states—Washington, Idaho, Montana, and Minnesota—also harvest a few. The depressed fur prices that helped the lynx repopulate historical ranges have disappeared. With an *average* lynx pelt worth about three hundred fifty dollars, there is some concern that trapping pressure during times of low lynx numbers could deal a serious blow to the lynx population. For now, however, there appear to be plenty of cats living in traditional lynx habitat. And Canadian provincial governments have reduced the lynx harvest in recent years, especially when cat populations are low.

Because lynx survive best in the deep and impenetrable northern woods, less is known about their territorial requirements. Estimates of home range size vary from six to nineteen square miles. Though they are less accepting of human presence than either the cougar or bobcat, there is some evidence that lynx may be more tolerant of their own kind. Still, they are essentially solitary hunters, and any group of lynx traveling together is likely to be made up of a female and her young.

Above all else, the lynx is a hunter, the only large predator capable of operating in the mature coniferous forests of the wintered north. They prey almost exclusively on snowshoe hares, with each cat killing one of the rodents about every other day. Grouse, mice, squirrels, deer, and caribou fawns round out the lynx's menu, but it is the snowshoe hare that keeps the lynx alive. Typically, a lynx travels more than a mile between kills.

When a lynx hunts alone, the procedure is invariably the same: Locate a hare by sight or sound. If the distance is not too great, rush in for the kill. If necessary, stalk close, then pounce. Despite its predatory prowess, a single lynx may need to pursue four or five hares before killing one. Because the hares they hunt travel along well-used trails, lynx have learned to wait in ambush for their prey. On average, though, the odds always favor the hare.

The chances of a kill increase dramatically on the frequent occasions when a female with her nearly grown young hunt together. Fanning out as they move through the forest, the cats often are able to chase an escaping hare into the jaws of another lynx. Of course, one hare will not feed four lynx, so the hunt must continue until all have eaten.

Gerry Parker, a Canadian biologist, happened across yet another hunting technique, albeit one with little promise. Reading the story from tracks in the snow, he discovered one orphaned juvenile lynx whose technique it was to dash suddenly

under snow-laden fir boughs even though it had not detected prey. A bit farther down the trail, it would repeat the blind attack. In the absence of its mother's training, the young cat probably had learned this technique early in its life when it made a dash under a tree and stumbled onto a hare. As far as Parker could tell, though, it never caught anything this way again.

One thing the lynx does not do well is run. Like other cats, it lacks the stamina necessary to wear prey down. If the lynx does not catch its quarry quickly, it gives up and moves on. On hard ground, even humans can outrun the cat over a long distance. And, supposedly, a man on snowshoes can capture a lynx even in deep snow if he's able to startle it into bounding away instead of trotting. When the lynx bounds, it sinks deep into the snow and soon becomes exhausted. Or so the theory goes.

The lynx has few natural enemies. Its ability to climb trees and travel through deep snow keep it safe from most predators, except on the rare occasions when wolves or a cougar catch it on hard ground and away from trees. Also, a few probably die from encounters with porcupines. But death sometimes comes in strange ways. A trapper once reported watching a lynx stalk a beaver that was slipping into and out of the water through a hole in the ice. When the beaver emerged from the water, the lynx sprang from behind a log and latched onto its prey just as the beaver dove into the water. To the trapper's great surprise, the beaver pulled the lynx into the water and out of sight under the ice. He waited for the cat to surface, but it did not. Later, the man used a forked pole to retrieve the drowned lynx from under the ice.

The animal that has by far the greatest impact on the lynx is the snowshoe hare it hunts. In one of the closest, best documented, most unwavering relationships in the wild world, the lynx and the hare are inextricably bound together. Because the lynx is the sole predator capable of matching the hare's ability to move over deep snow, it long ago forsook nearly all other prey and hitched its star to the hare. Unlike the bobcat, an opportunistic generalist that will take almost any kind of prey, the lynx is a specialist, feeding almost exclusively on hares. And as the hare goes, so goes the lynx.

Frontier trappers did not ply their trade long in North America before they noticed that the number of lynx they caught rose and fell like waves on the sea. Each period of lynx abundance seemed to be followed by several years of declining populations, culminating with an extreme scarcity of lynx. Then, gradually, cat numbers climbed again to a new peak, only to fall once more. The purchase records of Hudson's Bay Company, the major fur

Opposite: Fresh winter snow is no impediment to the lynx.

buyer, clearly documented this perplexing phenomenon, which typically ran about ten years from peak to peak.

It also was known that hares underwent similar periodic booms and busts. But ecologists did not fully connect the two and document their relationship until well into this century. When charted on paper, the increases and declines in lynx populations matched perfectly those of the hare. A year or two after hare numbers peaked, so would the lynx. When hare populations dropped, lynx declines were right behind. Soon after, when the hares bottomed out and began a recovery, so would the lynx.

It took scientists a while to understand fully the unusual relationship between the two species, but eventually they determined that it works like this: When hares are abundant, lynx become prolific, producing three to six young per year with little kit mortality. Then a food shortage, disease, or some genetic factor (almost certainly not lynx predation) intervenes, and the hare population plummets. With food scarce, lynx numbers decline. Eventually, however, hare density increases, and lynx prosperity follows. The cycle repeats itself about every ten years.

Because a female lynx almost certainly feeds herself before she feeds her young, the first fatalities of a reduced hare supply seem to be the kittens, which may starve outright or die from sibling aggression or disease. Females apparently continue to breed and conceive regardless of the food supply, although poor nutrition may cause them to abort or to reabsorb the fetuses. At some point in the hare decline, it simply becomes impossible for lynx to raise young.

Modern researchers say adult lynx probably don't die from starvation very often. But early naturalists, such as Ernest T. Seton, spoke of seeing "a dozen lynxes that were dying of starvation . . . and in the silent woods. . . a dozen shriveled corpses, muffled in the towseld wool that had been the superb winter coat of a lynx." A food shortage also can make the cats more vulnerable to trapping and may force them into conflicts with humans, as the lynx turn to domestic animals and carrion for food. When the hares disappear from one area, adult cats strike out in search of greener pastures, sometimes ending up in such non-traditional lynx range as the grasslands of southern Alberta and North Dakota. Occasionally, a few may be found as far south as Iowa, and they have been known to wander into towns in search of food.

In 1962-63 and again in the early 1970s, lynx wandered out of the woods and into the major cities of Edmonton and Calgary, Alberta, and Winnipeg, Manitoba. They also have been killed in the Minneapolis area, nearly two hundred miles south of their normal breeding range. The all-time distance champion, however, was a Yukon

Lynx kittens are as appealing
as their domestic counterparts.

lynx that traveled five hundred miles in a straight line in seven months after the local hare population crashed. And it might have gone even farther had it not ended up in a trap.

It is probably the lynx's solitary nature that long ago tied it inextricably to the snowshoe hare. Had the cat, like the wolf, learned to hunt with others of its kind, its diet might have broadened to include the moose and caribou that are much easier for a pack to bring down. But a single cat is capable of killing only smaller prey, and during northern winters, that usually means the snowshoe hare.

The epic relationship between lynx and hare can affect other species too. A couple decades ago on Newfoundland, resource managers noted that many caribou calves were dying from infected abscesses, usually on their necks. In some years, as many as seventy percent of the calves were lost, and the infection became the major factor limiting the growth of the island's caribou herd. The losses seemed to come in a cyclical pattern that took several years to complete, but no one knew what was causing the mortality.

Then one spring, a dead calf was found with four puncture wounds in its neck. Officials surmised that abscesses on previous dead calves may have hidden similar punctures, and a search was launched to find the cause of the wounds. Someone located the skull of a lynx, the largest predator on the island, and the canine teeth fit perfectly into the wounds.

Additional tests proved that lynx were indeed responsible, even though the cat was not a major caribou predator anywhere else in Canada. Later studies showed that the cycle of caribou deaths was closely related to the abundance of hares on the island. When hare numbers dropped, the lynx turned to young caribou for food. When hares became abundant, caribou predation declined. With the lynx as a sort of "middleman," the hares were controlling the caribou population.

Arthur Bergerud, one of the researchers who unraveled the mystery, reports that lynx now kill fewer caribou calves on Newfoundland. "The lynx population on the island has declined," he writes, "as a result of another cyclical phenomenon: women's fashions. Long-haired animal pelts have become fashionable, trapping lynx has become economically rewarding, and the density of lynx on Newfoundland has dropped."

Though being a furbearer and predator is deadly serious business, there's some evidence that lynx do take time to play. On forays through the woods, they often bound off the trail for no apparent reason. And during his study in Nova Scotia, Gerry Parker found that two or more of the cats often met in open bogs to romp about in what can only be described as play activity.

Occasionally, the cats even seem to enjoy toy-

Like most cats, these lynx demonstrate a fascination with moving water.

Learning by observation.

ing with the humans who enter their domain. Though lynx never attack humans, trappers have reported that the cats frequently follow them about the woods. "Often, the signal I receive from a lynx with a radio collar indicates that it is extremely close," says one researcher. "Then I turn and see the animal sitting on a rock watching me. I'm often unsure about just who is following whom."

Cape Breton Island

Though trappers and biologists have long known that the lynx and bobcat divided the North American continent roughly in half—lynx to the north and bobcats to the south—no one knew why. Why should two animals so similar not occupy the same terrain? Or, if they cannot live together, why doesn't one of them come to dominate all of the available habitat? What imaginary wall keeps them separate? Answers to these questions appear to lie on Cape Breton Island in the Canadian province of Nova Scotia.

Nova Scotia is a long, narrow maritime province lying in the Atlantic to the east of Maine. The northern third of Nova Scotia is an island, Cape Breton, which is cut off from the mainland by the Strait of Canso, three-quarters of a mile wide. Cape Breton has two distinct types of terrain. Most of the island is lowland: rolling, undulating hills covered with mixed broadleaf and coniferous forests. The elevated northwest portion of the island, however, rises abruptly as much as nine hundred feet above the lowland. On this high plateau, the land is covered by fir and spruce forests broken by peat bogs.

Historically, lynx have been the predominant feline on Cape Breton. For centuries, they prowled throughout the island from coastline to mountaintop with little competition for the prey they sought. There were no bobcats on the island, although they existed in other parts of the province.

In 1957, however, the government built a bridge across the Strait of Canso, providing a highway and rail link between Cape Breton and the rest of Nova Scotia. Cars and trains were not all that crossed the bridge, and it was not long before bobcats began showing up on Cape Breton. As they bred and multiplied there, a curious division of territory began to take place, a division not unlike the one that occurs all across southern Canada. In the lowlands, the thriving lynx population plummeted, and the bobcats prospered. But the high plateau remained virtually free of bobcats, and there the lynx retained its position of dominance.

Fascinated by this phenomenon, biologist Gerry Parker went looking for answers. In the late 1970s and early 1980s, he captured, radio collared, and tracked both cats, looking into every aspect of their lifestyles and their relationships with each other. Though his studies are not conclusive, he has formed some theories that might explain the curious division of territory that keeps the cats apart on Cape Breton and elsewhere.

First, there is the biological dictum that the closer two species resemble each other, the less tolerant they are of one another. When they try to fill the same niche, there's likely to be a conflict. But this does not come close to explaining the mutual exclusivity of the two cats, especially on Cape Breton where hares and other prey animals were plentiful. Though the bobcat is a more aggressive predator, it did not come to dominate the island's lower region by taking food out of the lynx's mouth.

Yet, the bobcat's temperament probably is the key. Parker believes that Cape Breton lynx were driven into the highlands by the bobcat's feisty personality. Though few—if any—people have ever witnessed a fight between the two cats, many researchers who have studied them believe the bobcat would indeed come out on top in such a confrontation. Contrary to the situation in most places, Cape Breton bobcats slightly outweigh the lynx there, adding credence to this theory. But even in areas where lynx typically are the larger animal, it's believed that the aggressive nature of the bobcat probably would carry the day.

Again, no one knows for sure what a confrontation between the two might look like, but Parker guesses that it may simply be a matter of two cats meeting in the woods, the bobcat subtly or overtly asserting its dominance, and the lynx slinking off to hunt some other territory. Knock down, drag out fights probably don't occur, but the lynx gets the message nonetheless.

Assuming that the bobcat's aggressive personality is what keeps the lynx out of the Cape Breton lowlands—and out of most of the continental United States—what, then, prevents the bobcat from moving north and ousting the lynx wherever it occurs? In the thirty years that bobcats have been on Cape Breton, they have not been able to establish themselves in the highlands. And in the eons they have roamed this continent, they have been unable to live in the far north. Why? Again, it appears that the answer can be found on Cape Breton.

A few years ago, Gerry Parker tested the theory he had formulated to explain this situation. He collected lynx and bobcat paws from professional trappers and attached the appendages to a spring-loaded gauge. He pressed each paw into the snow, noting on the gauge the amount of pressure it took to break through. The results: on snow, a lynx paw has about twice the supporting capacity of a bobcat paw. Because of the difference in elevation, Cape Breton's highlands receive much more snow than the adjacent lowlands. It's Parker's theory that the lynx dominates the highlands—and

Large feet keep the lynx on top of the snow.

Ghostlike, the lynx drifts through snow and mist.

the great expanse of Canadian northland as well—because it has the footgear to travel in deep snow. The bobcat does not.

The difference is striking. Because the two cats are about the same size, one might expect them to have the same size feet, but that is not the case. As noted earlier, the bobcat's feet are like those of a housecat, only proportionately larger. The lynx's foot, however, may be twice as large as a bobcat's, sometimes spreading to more than four inches in diameter. To human eyes they appear ridiculously large, comically out of proportion. In the winter, extra fur appears between the lynx's toes and around the edges of its paws. When the cat spreads its toes, fur fills the gaps and turns each foot into a very effective snowshoe. This subtle physiological advantage may be the major reason for the lynx's success in the north.

AFTERWORD

"The future of North America's great cats. . ."

The future of North America's great wild felines is in our hands. Biologists have exploded the myth that predators are evil vermin that must be destroyed. Ecologists understand what food and territory the cats need to survive. Economists know to the penny what a lynx skin or mounted cougar head is worth. Now, politicians and wildlife managers must be told about the aesthetic value of a wild cat no one may ever see. They need to know that habitat destruction and overtrapping must cease. They need to hear that you and I hold as high treasure the knowledge that somewhere out in the nearby woods prowls a great sinewy cat, the zenith of predatory evolution and the epitome of raw power perfectly controlled. It's our job to tell them. Yours and mine.

GARY TURBAK, a native of South Dakota, is a full-time freelance writer whose work has appeared in *Equinox, Reader's Digest, Field and Stream, National* and *International Wildlife, Writer's Digest,* and many other widely circulated periodicals. In addition, he has published two non-fiction books. On a more personal note, he is also a Viet Nam veteran. a cat lover, a former teacher, a professional photographer, and a life-long student of wildlife. Turbak and his wife live in Missoula, Montana.

ALAN CAREY is a professional wildlife photographer whose work has appeared in such publications as *National Wildlife, Smithsonian,* and *National Geographic World.* His love of wildlife and his desire to photograph America's animals and birds in their natural habitats have taken him from the Florida Everglades to the frozen Alaskan tundra. He lives with his wife and children in Montana.